DEADLY DISEASES

EBOLA

BY TAMMY GAGNE

CONTENT CONSULTANT
Michael Smit, MD, MSPH
Pediatric Infectious Diseases Physician
Children's Hospital Los Angeles

Cover image: The Ebola virus has a long, twisting shape that folds back on itself.

Core Library

An Imprint of Abdo Publishing
abdobooks.com

abdobooks.com

Published by Abdo Publishing, a division of ABDO, PO Box 398166, Minneapolis, Minnesota 55439.
Copyright © 2022 by Abdo Consulting Group, Inc. International copyrights reserved in all countries.
No part of this book may be reproduced in any form without written permission from the publisher.
Core Library™ is a trademark and logo of Abdo Publishing.

Printed in the United States of America, North Mankato, Minnesota.
102021
012022

THIS BOOK CONTAINS
RECYCLED MATERIALS

Cover Photo: Kateryna Kon/Shutterstock Images
Interior Photos: Michael Duff/AP Images, 4–5; Sally Hayden/SOPA Images/Shutterstock Images, 7;
Joe Giddens/PA Wire/AP Images, 8; Jerome Delay/AP Images, 11, 39, 40; Fabian Plock/Shutterstock
Images, 14–15; Philippe Psaila/Science Source, 17, 45; Red Line Editorial, 19; Thammanoon
Khamchalee/Shutterstock Images, 22; Scott Camazine/Science Source, 24–25, 43; Monica Schroeder/
Science Source, 26; Sunday Alamba/AP Images, 28; Nati Harnik/AP Images, 30; Jerome Delay/AP/
Shutterstock, 32–33; Pablo Martinez Monsivais/AP Images, 37

Editor: Arnold Ringstad
Series Designer: Ryan Gale

Library of Congress Control Number: 2021941192

Publisher's Cataloging-in-Publication Data

Names: Gagne, Tammy, author.
Title: Ebola / by Tammy Gagne
Description: Minneapolis, Minnesota : Abdo Publishing, 2022 | Series: Deadly diseases | Includes
    online resources and index.
Identifiers: ISBN 9781532196584 (lib. bdg.) | ISBN 9781098218393 (ebook)
Subjects: LCSH: Ebola virus disease--Juvenile literature. | Ebola hemorrhagic fever--Juvenile
    literature. | Infectious diseases--Juvenile literature. | Epidemics--History--Juvenile literature. |
    Communicable diseases--Epidemiology--Juvenile literature.
Classification: DDC 614.49--dc23

CONTENTS

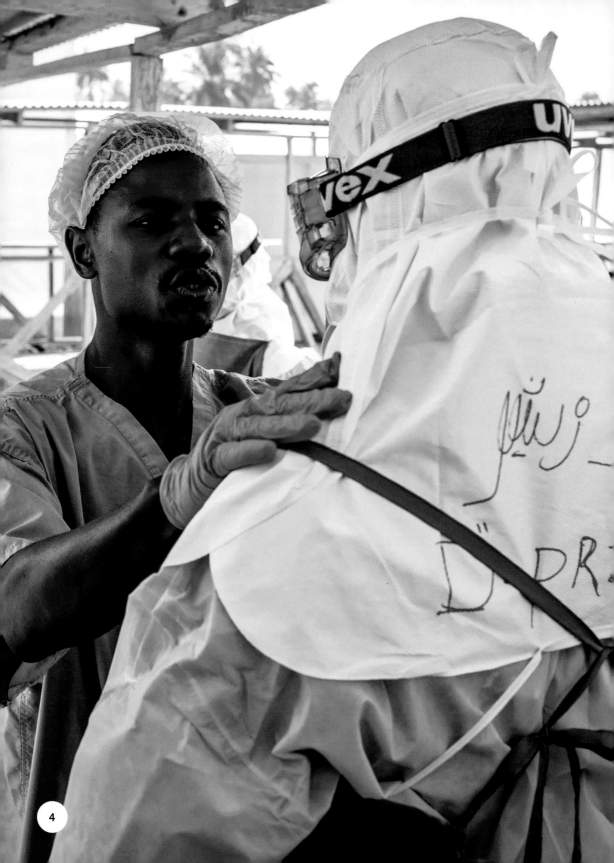

SURVIVING EBOLA

ugenie Kahambu Kiyora is a nurse in the Democratic Republic of the Congo (DRC). Health-care workers there are at risk of being exposed to a deadly illness called Ebola. This virus is rare. But several outbreaks have occurred in Africa. The illness is contagious and often deadly. About half the people who catch the virus die from it.

Many risks come with a career in caring for the sick. Still, Kiyora decided to work with patients with Ebola. Some were in the early

Being in an area affected by Ebola can be frightening and stressful for both residents and health-care workers.

stages of the illness. Many of these people had a fever, headache, or chills. Patients in later stages would cough or vomit blood. In 2018, a major outbreak of the disease began. Kiyora watched people die from Ebola each day. Her work wasn't easy, but she knew she was making a difference. She tried hard to save every patient she could.

When she wasn't at work, Kiyora spent time with her new husband. Shortly after they married, she was diagnosed with Ebola herself. She had caught it from one of the patients in her care. Kiyora was scared when she received her test results. She didn't know what her future would hold.

ARE SURVIVORS IMMUNE TO EBOLA?

Scientists think people who survive Ebola develop immunity to the virus. This means they are protected from catching it again. Some evidence suggests survivors may be immune to the disease for ten or more years. It is possible that they remain immune for the rest of their lives. Scientists continue to study Ebola immunity.

Nurses play key roles in helping communities during Ebola outbreaks.

MOVING BEYOND FEAR

Fortunately Kiyora did not die from the terrible illness. She was grateful. Kiyora knew that many other Ebola patients were not so lucky. But she was still worried after she recovered. Although Ebola has existed for decades, researchers are still learning about the way it works. Kiyora wondered whether she would get sick again. She might not survive a second battle with the illness.

She also worried about how other people might treat her. Some former Ebola patients say they face severe stigma from society. Many people don't want to be near others who have had Ebola. Kiyora experienced this stigma firsthand. Her neighbors worried about getting infected.

Kiyora was scared to return to work at first. But she eventually decided that what mattered most was helping others. She had taken an oath to do

PERSPECTIVES
BEING THERE FOR PATIENTS

Ebola patients are often lonely. The disease is too contagious for family and friends to be nearby. Having dedicated caregivers can make patients feel less alone. Kamala Kahindo is a nurse who survived Ebola. Now she works to help other Ebola patients. She says, "I wanted to help others. I know how hard it is. The fear of death doesn't stop haunting you. Sometimes a patient is so discouraged that they can't do anything for themselves. I become their friend."

Health-care workers must wear special gear to stay safe during outbreaks of Ebola.

just that. She knew her work required courage. She also knew it offered her a great deal of joy. Her coworkers welcomed her back. Together they continued to save every life they could.

IS EBOLA STILL SPREADING?

For most people the risk of catching Ebola is low. Outbreaks do still occur. But to get the virus, a person must touch fluids from an infected person. These include blood, saliva, sweat, diarrhea, and vomit. Health-care workers and family members usually face the highest risk.

Being careful can greatly reduce the chances of getting sick. Wearing gowns and gloves is important. It is also essential that caregivers not touch their own faces or bodies without disinfecting after working with a patient. The virus can enter a person's body through the eyes, nose, mouth, or wounds in the skin. Caregivers must wash their hands often to reduce that risk.

People must be very careful when handling the body of a person who has died from Ebola.

Although Ebola is rare, uncontrolled outbreaks can overwhelm communities. Teaching the public about Ebola has been the best way to slow the spread. People suffering from Ebola should be kept in isolation. When a patient dies, it is important that loved ones not touch the body. Even after a patient dies, the virus can be passed on if the body is touched.

The outbreak that sickened Kiyora was neither the first nor the last in the DRC. The following year, the nation's eleventh outbreak began in May. The DRC and the World Health Organization (WHO) officially declared the outbreak over on November 18, 2020. Everyone remains on the lookout for new cases. Health-care workers are ready to contain future outbreaks.

STRAIGHT TO THE
SOURCE

Adaora Okoli survived Ebola. The experience left her with a desire to study medicine. Okoli wanted to help people in her native country, Nigeria. She said:

> When I got sick with Ebola and I was sent into the isolation room with the other people that were ill with me, we only had one infectious disease specialist who was taking care of us the first week and he was a foreigner. . . . I realized it's so easy to not really know what the patient is feeling. So I'm more empathic. It really did open my eyes to the fact that infectious disease is a disease of poverty, and countries that have very limited resources are not able to contain the diseases quickly. . . . We don't have a lot of infectious disease specialists in Nigeria who know what to do when this sort of thing happens, which is dangerous.

Source: Wilborn P. Nobles III. "A Tulane Student Survived Ebola. Now She Is Bill Gates' Hero." *NOLA*, 12 July 2019, nola.com. Accessed 6 May 2021.

BACK IT UP

The speaker is using evidence to support a point. Write a paragraph describing the point she is making. Then write down two or three pieces of evidence she uses to make the point.

THE HISTORY OF EBOLA

In 1976 an unknown disease began spreading in two African countries. The first people to become sick lived in Yambuku, Zaire. This country would later be renamed the Democratic Republic of the Congo. A second outbreak took place about 500 miles (805 km) away in Nzara, in what is now South Sudan. Doctors called the mysterious illness a type of hemorrhagic fever. The word *hemorrhagic* means bleeding. Many people with the illness bled from their eyes,

The Democratic Republic of the Congo, then known as Zaire, was the site of the earliest Ebola outbreak.

ears, or mouths. Doctors soon discovered internal bleeding in many patients as well.

Scientists began investigating the illness. They needed to figure out how it was spreading. This could help them stop it. They also had to give the illness an official name. One of the scientists suggested naming the disease after Yambuku. Diseases had been named this way in the past. But another scientist thought this was a bad idea. He worried that it would attach a stigma to the village. The leader of the group then suggested naming the illness Ebola. This was the name of a nearby river.

At first scientists thought the illness had spread from one country to the other. They suspected an infected person had traveled from Yambuku to Nzara. But their research showed this wasn't the case. Instead two similar viruses had emerged around the same time. Doctors named them *Zaire ebolavirus* and *Sudan*

Scientists did research to learn more about the Ebola virus and how it works.

ebolavirus. These viruses, along with four others that were later discovered, cause Ebola virus disease.

Ebola was a dangerous illness. By the end of the outbreak in Yambuku, 318 people had become infected. Of them, 280 died. The numbers in Nzara were also grim. Of the 284 people who caught the illness there, 151 did not survive.

MORE EBOLA CASES

Ebola cases kept occurring in the years that followed. Most were in Africa. For nearly two decades, the outbreaks were small but deadly. Nzara faced a second outbreak in 1979. This time 34 people in that town and the nearby city of Yambio fell ill. By the time that outbreak ended, 22 patients had died. In 1995 Ebola also returned to the DRC. This outbreak was almost as large as the country's first one. There were 315 reported cases and 254 deaths.

For another decade, outbreaks continued in Africa. Again, most were small. In many cases the death counts were in the single digits. But the fight against Ebola was far from over. Uganda had two larger outbreaks during this time. The country reported 425 cases in 2000. There were another 131 in 2007.

The largest Ebola outbreak in history began in 2014. It lasted more than two years. The outbreak began in southeastern Guinea. It then spread to Liberia

EBOLA VIRUS
OUTBREAKS

Ebola outbreaks have occurred in 13 African countries since 1976. The first outbreak occurred in the DRC, which was then known as Zaire. It was also where an outbreak happened in 2020. How does this map help you understand the impact of Ebola?

Senegal

Mali

South Sudan

Guinea

Nigeria

Sierra Leone

Liberia

Gabon

Côte d'Ivoire

Congo

Uganda

Democratic Republic of the Congo

South Africa

WHY DIDN'T EBOLA SPREAD?

Some people wondered why Ebola did not spread across the world like COVID-19 did. People with COVID-19 can spread it to others before developing any symptoms. Some people never have symptoms. But by the time Ebola patients can pass their illness to others, most are too sick to leave their beds. This makes it less likely for them to spread Ebola to others.

and Sierra Leone. For this reason it is often called the West African Ebola epidemic. About 28,600 people became infected with Ebola between 2014 and 2016. A total of 11,308 died. Health-care workers from many countries stepped up to treat the sick. They also tried to contain the disease.

ONGOING OUTBREAKS

Ebola remains a threat to the health of people in many African nations. In early 2021 outbreaks were ongoing in the DRC and Guinea. However, by this time another virus had taken over most news headlines. The COVID-19 virus first appeared in Wuhan, China, in late 2019. The illness spread to every continent over the next year. By June 2021 more than 170 million people had become infected. More than 3 million had died from the virus.

Ebola has a much higher fatality rate than COVID-19. The fatality rate of COVID-19 was estimated to be around 1 to 3 percent in most countries. By contrast, Ebola may kill more than 50 percent of the people who catch it.

PERSPECTIVES
CHANGING CULTURES

Ebola has taken many lives. It has also changed the way survivors must live. Simple behaviors that were once big parts of everyday life are now seen as dangerous. Esaie Ngalya lives in the DRC. His grandmother died from Ebola there. The disease has made it necessary for his family to place safety ahead of their social customs. Ngalya said, "Ebola has changed our culture. Now I go to see my uncle but we don't shake hands. In our culture that is considered disrespectful but now we have no choice because health comes first."

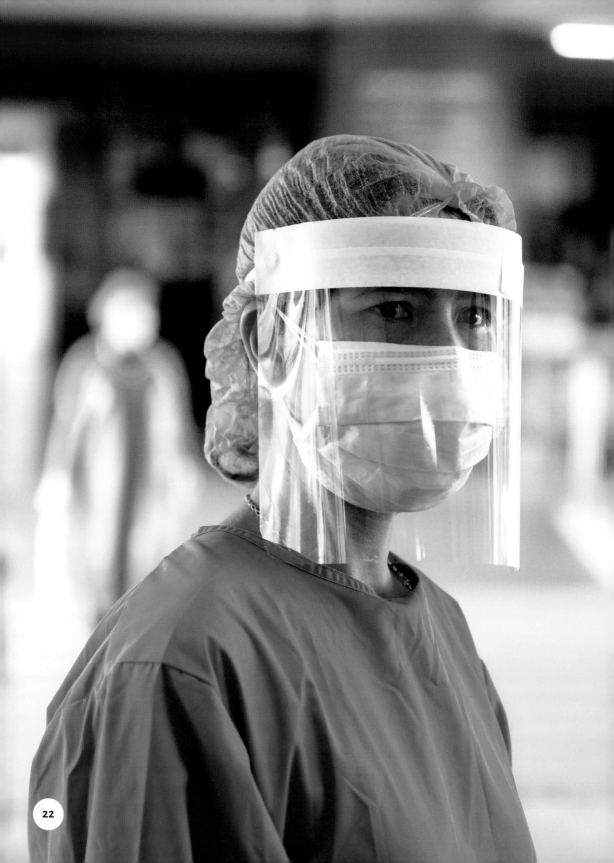

Some Ebola outbreaks have had fatality rates as high as 90 percent.

One thing the world learned from COVID-19 was that a delayed response costs lives. The pandemic showed the importance of giving health-care workers the resources they need. Many lives have been lost to both diseases.

FURTHER EVIDENCE

Chapter Two discusses how the Ebola virus has spread in the past. What was one of this chapter's main points? What evidence is included to support this point? Watch the video at the website below. Does the information on the website support this point? Does it present new evidence?

CONTACT TRACING

abdocorelibrary.com/ebola

As with Ebola, health-care workers dealing with COVID-19 needed special gear to keep themselves safe.

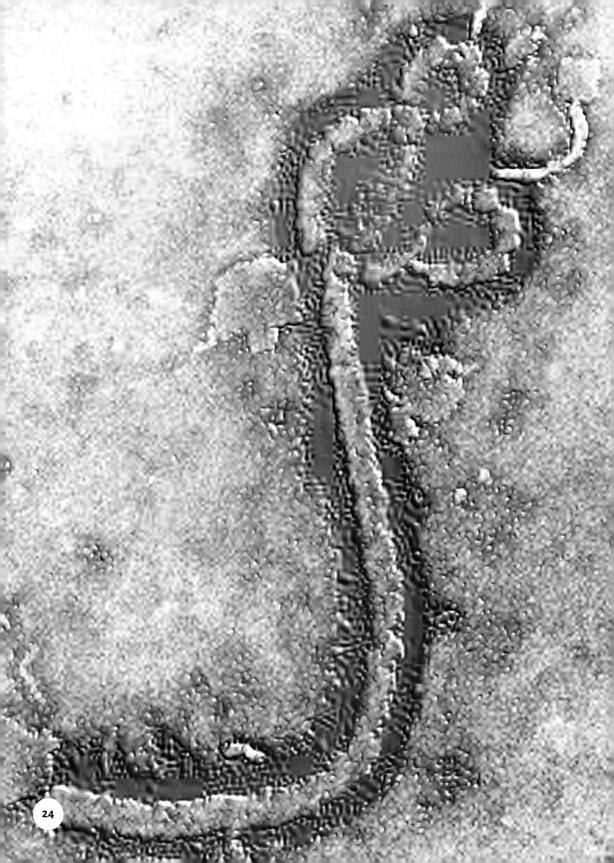

THE SCIENCE
OF EBOLA

V iruses are much too small to be seen by the naked eye. Scientists can view them only through powerful microscopes. Viruses come in different sizes and shapes. Most are shaped like rods or spheres. When scientists first saw the Ebola virus, they quickly noticed that it looked different. It wasn't round like a sphere. It also wasn't straight like a rod. Instead, it curved in places. It even wrapped around itself. It looked like a piece of string or a worm.

Scientists took the first-ever photo of the Ebola virus through a powerful microscope in October 1976.

THE SCALE OF THE
EBOLA VIRUS

Viruses, including Ebola, are amazingly small. This diagram compares the sizes of the Ebola virus and a few other tiny things, like a red blood cell, bacteria, and other viruses. What does this image suggest about the challenges of studying the Ebola virus?

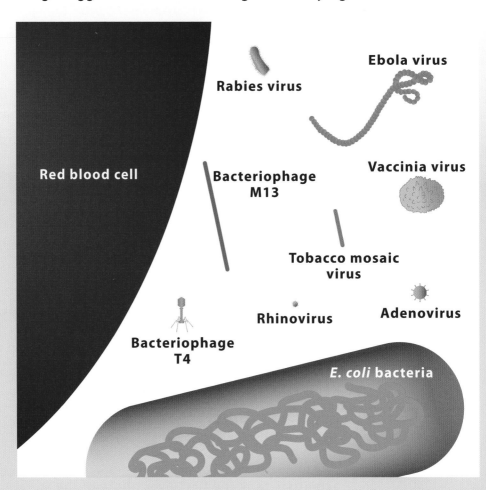

Rabies virus

Ebola virus

Red blood cell

Bacteriophage
M13

Vaccinia virus

Tobacco mosaic
virus

Rhinovirus

Adenovirus

Bacteriophage
T4

E. coli bacteria

It measured just 80 nanometers in diameter. This is about 1,000 times thinner than a human hair.

For something so tiny, a virus can be extremely dangerous. But it needs a host to survive. A virus may use the cells of an animal or plant for this purpose. The virus takes over these cells. Once a virus invades a host, it begins to replicate. This means it makes copies of itself. Those copies can then invade more cells.

HOW EBOLA SPREADS

As a virus replicates in a human body, the host usually becomes sick. The host can then pass the virus to other people. They become infected too. The timeline for when a person becomes

REMAINING THE SAME

Over time many viruses mutate. This means they undergo changes when they replicate. Some mutations cause a virus to become more contagious. But Ebola has not mutated much at all. It is 97 percent identical to the virus that first emerged in 1976. This has made it easier for disease experts to contain Ebola.

Washing hands is an important part of staying safe from Ebola.

contagious varies by virus. People with Ebola can start spreading it as soon as they develop symptoms.

Different viruses spread in different ways. Some remain in the air after an infected person has coughed or sneezed. Other viruses can survive for short periods of time on surfaces. The Ebola virus spreads through direct contact with the blood or other body fluids of an infected person. It can also spread through contact with objects that have touched these fluids. These objects can include bedding or medical equipment such as needles.

Humans are not the only animals that can become infected with Ebola. Bats and nonhuman primates can be infected too. If a person contacts the body fluids of an infected animal, the human can catch the disease.

The general public faces little risk of catching Ebola. People cannot catch the illness through casual

PERSPECTIVES
COULD EBOLA BECOME A BIGGER PROBLEM?

No one knows for sure where Ebola came from. Many scientists think that it came from an animal such as a bat or a nonhuman primate. The animal then likely infected a human being. However, humans pass most cases of Ebola to other people. This spread between humans could allow the illness to become more contagious. Dr. Robert Garry researches Ebola at Tulane University. He explains, "It's going to change. A human being is not a bat. The longer this virus is allowed to propagate human to human, the more it is going to adapt."

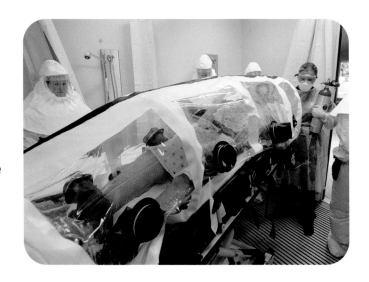

Patients with Ebola need quick medical attention, but health-care workers must also make sure to stay safe.

contact. Those most at risk for the disease are family members and health-care workers who care for people with the illness. Using proper safety equipment such as masks, gloves, and gowns helps prevent transmission. Caregivers must know how to remove these items safely after working. If they do not do it properly, their risk of catching the disease rises.

EBOLA SYMPTOMS

Signs of Ebola may appear between two and twenty-one days after contact with the virus. This time between exposure and the first symptoms is called the incubation period. Most commonly, the incubation period is eight to ten days. The disease often starts with a sudden fever, headache, and sore throat. The patient may feel weakness along with joint and muscle pain.

Most patients also develop stomach pain. They may experience diarrhea and vomiting. They might lose interest in eating. Some people get a rash. The virus attacks the patient's internal organs. It weakens the immune system. Ebola also reduces the body's ability to clot blood. If bleeding begins, it can be hard for health-care workers to stop it. In the worst cases, patients can bleed to death.

EXPLORE ONLINE

The focus of Chapter Three is on the science of the Ebola virus. The website below focuses on the same topic. As you know, every source is different. How is the information at the website different from the information in this chapter? What information is the same? What information did you learn from the website?

EBOLA 101

abdocorelibrary.com/ebola

TREATING EBOLA

Viruses cannot generally be cured with medication. Instead, health-care workers treat the symptoms as a virus runs its course. This is called supportive care. For Ebola this begins with giving the patient fluids with electrolytes. These are minerals that keep fluid levels balanced, help muscles work properly, and aid in blood clotting. Fever, diarrhea, and vomiting can severely lower the body's electrolytes.

Ebola causes a patient's oxygen levels and blood pressure to drop. For this reason

Health-care workers may set up isolation tents where they can safely treat Ebola patients.

health-care workers often give patients supplemental oxygen and blood pressure medication. Caregivers also need to treat other infections that may arise. Because Ebola weakens the immune system, patients may have a hard time fighting other illnesses while battling Ebola.

In 2020 the first two drugs were approved to treat Ebola. They are called Inmazeb and Ebanga. These medications bind to the Ebola virus. This stops the virus from entering new cells. The virus cannot replicate. Studies have shown these drugs give Ebola patients a better chance of surviving the disease.

EBOLA'S AFTEREFFECTS

Surviving Ebola is a huge milestone. But many Ebola patients end up dealing with more health problems afterward. Eye problems, headaches, and joint pain are common following the disease. Other Ebola survivors feel tired, gain weight, or have stomach issues. The exact problems a former patient experiences vary. When they occur and how long they last also depend on the individual.

Scientists do not fully understand what causes these aftereffects. But they

SAYING GOOD-BYE SAFELY

People who lose loved ones to Ebola must be careful. The Ebola virus remains infectious even after its host is no longer alive. Funeral customs such as kissing or touching the dead are common in West Africa. But these behaviors can quickly pass the infection to the grieving family members.

do know that follow-up care can help. Former Ebola patients may suffer from vision problems. They may be sensitive to bright light. Some even lose their sight. But regular eye checkups and care can reduce these problems.

Getting regular medical care isn't always easy in some African nations. The World Health Organization (WHO) has created a program to help. It offers follow-up care to Ebola survivors. The program offers patients monthly visits for the first six months after their illness. It then offers visits every three months for the next year.

The program does not treat just physical health problems. Many survivors also experience anxiety, depression, and post-traumatic stress disorder. The WHO program also supports former Ebola patients by offering treatment for mental health issues like these.

Nurse Nina Pham caught Ebola after treating a patient at a Dallas, Texas, hospital. After getting better, she met with US public health official Dr. Anthony Fauci.

TESTING AND VACCINATING FOR EBOLA

Testing for Ebola has improved greatly since the virus was first discovered. Patients can now get results in just 15 minutes. This increases their chances for survival because they can start treatment sooner. Rapid testing also lowers the risk of patients spreading the disease while they wait for results.

In 2019 the US Food and Drug Administration approved the first Ebola vaccine. Even before this approval, the DRC began using it. The government approved emergency use of the vaccine to fight the ongoing outbreak. Between August 2018 and March 2020, more than 300,000 people in the DRC received the vaccine. It was a huge step in preventing Ebola virus disease. The vaccine is now licensed in the DRC. Five other African countries have also licensed it.

In 2019, Doctors Without Borders reported that not enough people were getting the Ebola vaccine. In February 2021, Ebola was once again emerging in

Dealing with the stress and fear of an Ebola outbreak can lead to mental health issues.

the DRC and Guinea. The WHO worked to slow the outbreak by treating the sick and vaccinating as many people as possible.

Ebola is still rare. But it remains a threat to many people in Africa. A major outbreak could also spread to other parts of the world. Education is the best weapon health-care workers have in stopping the disease.

A child in Uganda receives an Ebola vaccine in June 2019.

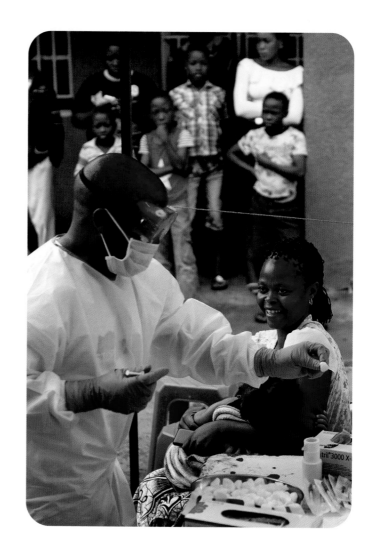

Knowing how to safely care for the sick is important. Getting the vaccine to as many people at risk as possible will also help. These steps will reduce the danger posed by the Ebola virus.

STRAIGHT TO THE
SOURCE

Ashoka Mukpo is a journalist who got Ebola while working in Liberia. During the COVID-19 pandemic, he felt people could learn a lot from past Ebola outbreaks. He said:

> *Viral outbreaks are frightening, but in a sense they also provide us with an opportunity. When we take precautions or try to hold our minds steady, we aren't just doing ourselves a favor, we are acting compassionately toward our neighbors and loved ones. Civic generosity and solidarity are vehicles that will get us to the other side of this unsettling time as fast as possible. And get to the other side we will. . . . Many will suffer before this all comes to an end. We owe it to them and one another to be as responsible and kind as we can, and to act in a way we will be proud of once it does.*

> Source: Ashoka Mukpo. "Lessons from an Ebola Survivor: Here's What We Can Do about the Coronavirus." *Boston Globe*, 16 Mar. 2020, bostonglobe.com. Accessed 6 May 2021.

WHAT'S THE BIG IDEA?

Take a close look at Mukpo's words. What is his main idea? What evidence is used to support his point? Write a few sentences showing how Mukpo uses evidence to support his main point.

IMPORTANT DATES

1976
Ebola emerges in Africa. Two separate outbreaks begin in what are now the Democratic Republic of the Congo (DRC) and South Sudan.

2000
Uganda has an Ebola outbreak with 425 cases.

2014
The largest Ebola outbreak in history begins. It is called the West African epidemic. About 28,600 people become infected, and 11,308 die.

2016
The West African epidemic ends.

2018
People in the DRC begin receiving the first Ebola vaccine following an emergency approval by their government.

2019
The US Food and Drug Administration approves the first Ebola vaccine.

2020
The first two drugs are approved to treat Ebola.

2021
In the midst of the COVID-19 pandemic, Ebola outbreaks continue in the DRC and Guinea.

STOP AND
THINK

Tell the Tale

Chapter One discusses a nurse who treated patients during an Ebola outbreak. Imagine that you are a nurse in a region where Ebola is spreading. Write 200 words about your experience. How important do you think nurses are during an outbreak such as this one?

Surprise Me

After reading this book, what two or three facts about the Ebola virus did you find most surprising? Write a few sentences about each fact. Why did you find each fact surprising?

Dig Deeper

After reading this book, what questions do you still have about Ebola? With an adult's help, find a few reliable sources that can help you answer your questions. Write a paragraph about what you learned.

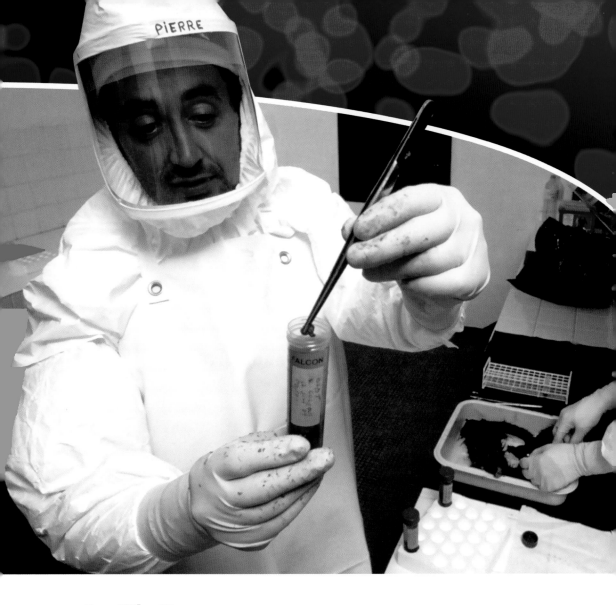

Say What?

Studying a deadly disease can mean learning a lot of new vocabulary. Find five words in this book you've never seen before. Use a dictionary to find out what they mean. Then write the meanings in your own words and use each word in a new sentence.

GLOSSARY

casual
relaxed, in passing

civic
related to the duties a person or group has to other people in society

clot
to form a thick mass

empathic
showing an ability to understand and share the feelings of another person

internal
inside the body

mutate
to change in form or nature

outbreak
a sudden rise in the occurrence of a disease

pandemic
a disease outbreak that spreads to many countries

propagate
to spread widely

replicate
to make a copy

solidarity
agreement of feeling or action among a group for a common cause

stigma
a negative association attached to a person or circumstance

ONLINE RESOURCES

To learn more about Ebola, visit our free resource websites below.

Visit **abdocorelibrary.com** or scan this QR code for free Common Core resources for teachers and students, including vetted activities, multimedia, and booklinks, for deeper subject comprehension.

Visit **abdobooklinks.com** or scan this QR code for free additional online weblinks for further learning. These links are routinely monitored and updated to provide the most current information available.

LEARN MORE

Bates, Mary. *Malaria*. Abdo, 2022.

Hand, Carol. *COVID-19*. Abdo, 2022.

Hudak, Heather C. *Ebola*. AV2, 2020.

INDEX

About the Author

Tammy Gagne has written hundreds of books for both adults and children. Some of her recent books have been about media literacy and mental health. She lives in northern New England with her husband, her son, and several pets.